# Helen Churchill Candee

# Jacobean Furniture

AF209183

Salzwasser

# Helen Churchill Candee

# Jacobean Furniture

1. Auflage | ISBN: 978-3-84604-850-4

Erscheinungsort: Frankfurt, Deutschland

Erscheinungsjahr: 2020

Salzwasser Verlag GmbH

Reprint of the original.

# JACOBEAN FURNITURE

# JACOBEAN FURNITURE

AND

## ENGLISH STYLES IN OAK AND WALNUT

BY

### HELEN CHURCHILL CANDEE

AUTHOR OF "DECORATIVE STYLES AND PERIODS,"
"THE TAPESTRY BOOK," ETC.

*WITH FORTY-THREE ILLUSTRATIONS*

NEW YORK
FREDERICK A. STOKES COMPANY
PUBLISHERS

# CONTENTS

# ILLUSTRATIONS

# ILLUSTRATIONS

# JACOBEAN FURNITURE

## CHAPTER I

### EARLY JACOBEAN STYLES

#### JAMES I CROWNED 1603

WHEN a passion for collecting antique furniture first swept America, and prizes were plucked from attics, cellars and old barns, the eagle eye of the amateur sought only those fine pieces that were made in the age of mahogany and satin-wood. Every piece was dubbed Colonial with rash generalisation until the time when a little erudition apportioned the well-made distinctive furniture to its proper classes. Then every person of culture became expert on eighteenth century furniture, and the names of Chippendale and his prolific mates fell glibly from all lips.

That much accomplished, the collector and home-maker then threw an intelligent eye on another page of history and realised that the seventeenth century and certain bits of oak and walnut that had stood neglected, belonged to an equally interesting period of America's social development.

All at once the word Jacobean was on every tongue, as Colonial had been before. Attics, cellars and barns were searched again, this time for oak and walnut, not mahogany, and for heavy square construction, not for bandy legs and delicate restraint. It was the marvellous carved chest that first announced itself, and then a six-legged highboy, and the lower part of a thousand-legged table—which now we call a gate. These, we said with inspiration, are the gods of the first settlers; mahogany is but modern stuff.

But this time we were more savant than before, and instead of starving our eager minds on the occasional resurrected American bit, we went at once to the source, to England, and there found in abundance (for the long purse) a charming sequence of styles covering all the times of our earlier history as settlers and colonisers. Thus were we able to identify these strange early pieces of our own and to recognise our quarry when found in a dusty corner.

That very old pieces still are found, pieces brought over here in the days of their mode, is proved to any collector. In two towns on Long Island Sound I recently found for sale two six-legged highboys, William and Mary, and that great rarity, a straight oak chair known as a Farthingale chair, made without arms for the purpose of accommodating the enormous crinoline or farthingale of its day. This chair may have supported the stiffly dressed ladies of

Plate II—LATE TUDOR MANTEL

From a house built in 1606, which shows a toning of Tudor style into Jacobean

Plate III—LATE TUDOR BED
With motifs which characterised early Jacobean carving, dated 1593

Elizabeth's court, so like it was to the Italian models of Tudor times.

The pity of it is, that no sooner had the artistic eye of the true collector begun to search for seventeenth century furniture than the commercial eye of the modern manufacturer began to make hideous variations on its salient features. He caught the name of Jacobean and to every piece of ill-drawn furniture he affixed a spiral leg and the Stuart name; or, he set a serpentine flat stretcher and called his mahogany dining set, William and Mary. These tasteless things fill our department stores, and it is they that are rapidly filling American homes. And the worst of it is, that both buyers and sellers are startlingly yet pathetically glib with attaching historic names to the mongrel stuff, and thus are they misled.

New furniture must be made, however, or resort must be had to soap-boxes and hammocks. The old models are the best to follow for the reason that the present is not an age of creation in this direction. The stylist is always a hobby-rider, and I must confess to that form of activity, but it is always with the idea in mind to make and keep our homes beautiful. And so I make the plea to manufacturers to stick to old models of tried beauty, and to buyers to educate their taste until they reject a hybrid or mongrel movable with the same outraged sense that they reject a mongrel dog.

Now let us pass through the gate that leads to

happy hunting-grounds of study where we find historic men and women, both royal and common, making the times that called for the furniture we now admire as deeply as they admired it.

One might almost say that since Henry the Eighth's introduction of the styles of the Italian Renaissance into England, that country has produced no original style of furniture. But lest this statement be resented by affronted savants and hurt sentimentalists, side by side with that fact must be placed another, that England has played upon the styles she imported with such skill and grace that she has thus produced variants of great and peculiar beauty.

England has taken the furniture creations of Europe through the centuries and has impressed them with her national traits, with a resulting beauty entirely her own. The effect is bewildering to all but the student of styles, for without study one is often unable to account for certain alterations of detail and construction. It cannot be too often repeated that as each nation in turn adopted the Italian Renaissance, that nation impressed its own signet upon the style. Thus came all the variations.

It is to be remembered that in the case of England, the affair is one of great interest and complication. In the sixteenth century Pistaccio and his artist mates hurried from Italy at the bidding of Henry VIII and planted their classic patterns in the British kingdom. That was an infusion of the pure

Plate IV—LARGE OAK CHEST
In noblest type of early Jacobean carving
*Courtesy of Charles*

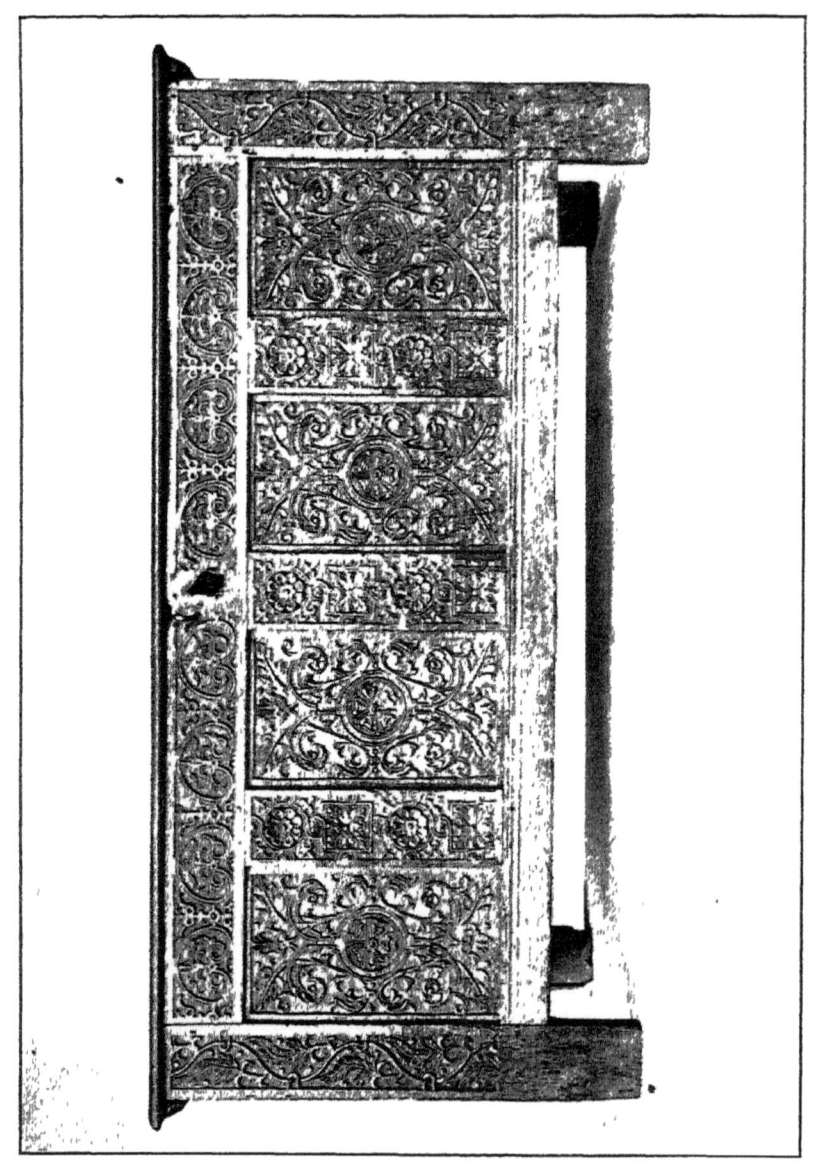

Plate V—EARLY JACOBEAN CHEST OF CARVED OAK

Renaissance drawing is visible but with a general flattening of the relief

blood of the Renaissance, and it lasted well into Elizabeth's time before the Anglo-Saxon temperament altered it characteristically.

By the time James I, in 1603, established the Stuart reign, the style became markedly British, and British styles called Jacobean in compliment to James' Latinized name, prevailed until another imported fashion came along. Then came another and another, and so on even until the end of Georgian styles and the beginning of Victorian.

The Jacobean style developed serenely, playing happy pranks with itself, altered by mechanical inventions and by new woods, until the second half of the seventeenth century, when Charles II introduced strong French influence and Portuguese—which was not greatly different from Spanish. The French influence came lightly from the light ladies of the frivolous court, and the Portuguese from Charles' queen, Catherine, whose home was Braganza. Bombay as her dowry threw Eastern colours and design into the mêlée.

British styles were not yet to be let alone, for no sooner was the French way set than the Dutch pattern appeared, brought over by William and Mary. Delicately it came at first, giving place for hints from the court of Louis XIV, and then in full force by the time Anne took the sceptre in 1703. And all these styles imported throughout the seventeenth century, what were they but the several interpretations of the Renaissance as it was expressed in France, Portugal, and Holland? Let not the student stagger under these complications of English styles, for although there are yet more reasons for the shapes and ornament of furniture in England during the seventeenth century they are all bright with incidents of kings and courts.

Tudor monarchs stop in 1603 at Elizabeth's death, but Tudor styles were not at once outgrown, rather they linger along far into the seventeenth century, heavily and elegantly regarding the newly throned Stuarts and their bewitching manners. The Tudor table, for instance, was a serious piece of furniture, put together as squarely and solidly as a house. Its enduring qualities are proved by the number of these tables still extant which, as refectory tables, are the smart thing for the dining-room of to-day. Bulbous legs with Italian carving, heavy square stretchers low on the ground, and draw-tops, are the distinguishing features. It is even suggested by the erudite that these tables are the last flicker of the style left by the Romans during their occupation of England, so like are they to pictured tables of Rome at that time.

To fix in the mind certain important motifs used in early Jacobean carving, a pause may be made before the fine oak bed pictured in Plate 3, that we may discuss them. It is dated 1593, ten years before James I, but, although Tudor, it has certain decora-

Plate VI—OAK CHEST WITH DRAWERS.

This is carved with all the characteristic motifs of early Jacobean work—the arch, the guilloche, the S curve in pairs

Plate VII—OAK STAND AND MARQUETRY CABINET
Here are combined the Jacobean robust strength and Spanish Moresque detail

tive features, the development of which was left to the Jacobean styles of the seventeenth century. Note especially among these the characteristic round arch savouring of the Norman, of which two are shown on the bed's head. These arches frame a rough inlay which appears also on the square blocks of the tester. Holly and bog oak were the favourite woods for this inlay on oak, woods obdurate enough to make the labour difficult. The half-circle repeat is used freely as a moulding on the headboard, and this develops in later furniture into an important motif. The general construction of this bed is noble in its proportions, and in all changes of fashion must it stand with the dignity of a temple.

As pictures on a screen melt one into another, so styles merge. Plate 6 shows a chest full of Jacobean promise yet retaining Tudor feeling. The fact that it has drawers under the coffer pronounces it as a novelty of the early seventeenth century, and therefore Jacobean.

It especially well illustrates the pattern for carving that occupied workers through the reign of James I. There is the Norman arch, low and wide, set on short supports which have now lost their architectural look of a column. The arches at the ends have as ornament the guilloche, that line of circles that sinuously proceeds through all that time. The carving just under the lid shows the characteristic S curve in one of its many varieties, and the line of decoration just above the drawers indicates the development of the half-circle. Thus are shown in this one early piece the principal motifs of the carvers who were coaxing the models of a past Renaissance into an expression that was entirely British.

The small oak cupboard on Plate 11 is another transition piece, being in feeling both Tudor and Jacobean. Here the guilloche is enlarged to form a panel ornament, and the acanthus becomes a long fern frond to ornament the uprights. One hardly feels, however, that this piece was ever the accompaniment of elegant living, although much antiquity gives its present distinction.

Continuing with the low round arch as an ornament in the low-relief carving of James' time, an example of its use is given in the folding gate-legged table which is the property of the author (Plate 8). The turned legs finished with squares, top and bottom, are characteristic of the first quarter of the century. The arch is here used as an apron to give elegance, and above is a drawer carved with leaves. In construction this table presents three sides to the front, as does the cabinet just considered, and its Italian inspiration is evident. Like all old oak of the time, it is put together with wooden pegs, and bears the marvellous patine of time.

Had the chairs of early Stuart time not been heavily made and squarely constructed we would not have had so many examples with which to gladden

Plate VIII—GATE-LEG TABLE, FORMING CONSOLE WITH GATE
CLOSED

The turned legs with square bases and tops indicate date as early as 1610   The
deep apron carved with fretted arch is an unusual feature

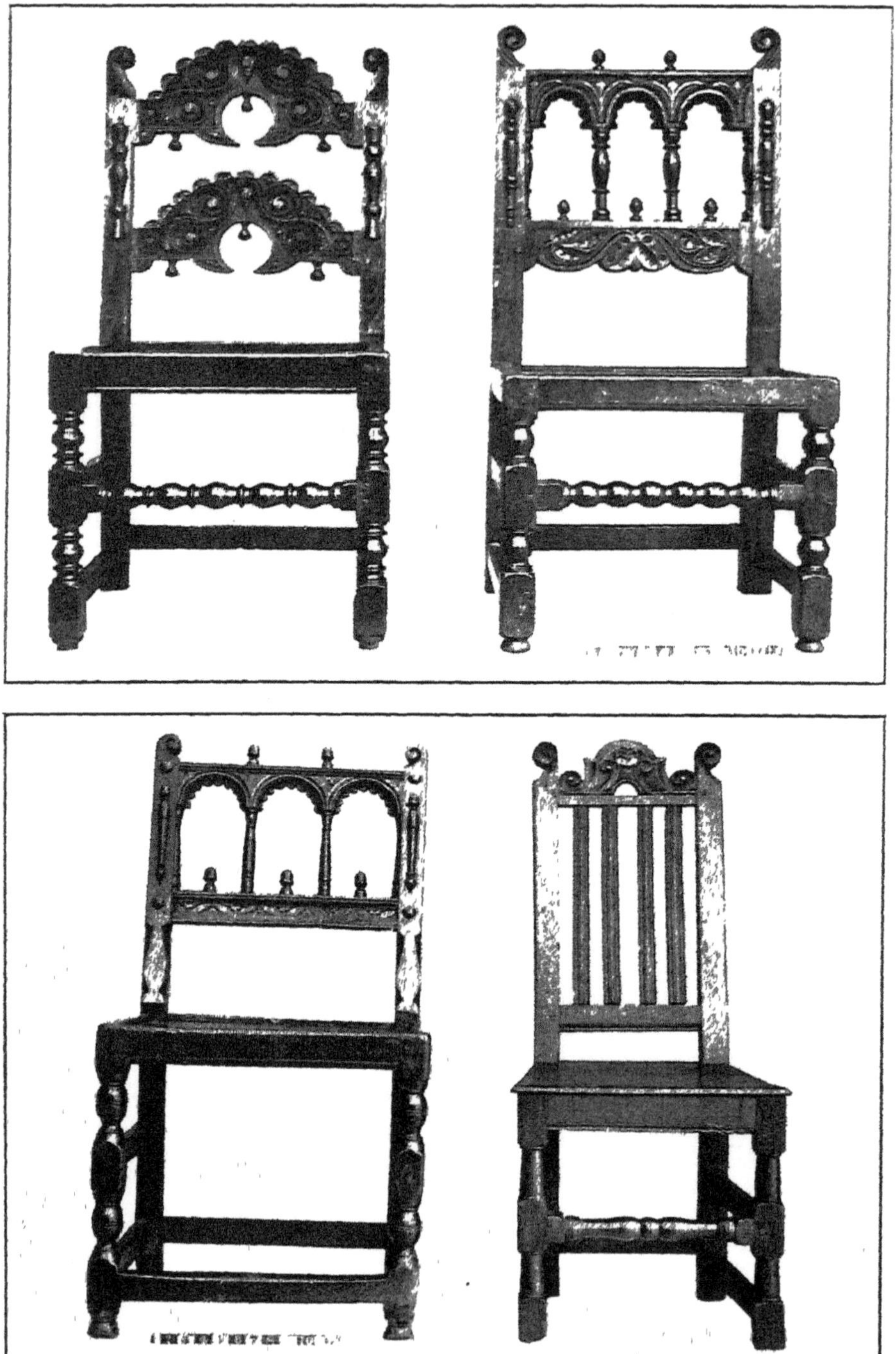

Plate IX—OAK CHAIRS
Early XVII Century Italian Inspiration

the eye. Almost without exception they are variants of the Italian, originality having not then appeared possible to chair makers. Three of the four chairs in the plates illustrate this so well that it is worth while to make a comparison with old Italian chairs.

The chair on Plate 9 with a screscent-shaped carving on the back had its first inspiration in Venice, that great port getting the idea from the wares of Constantinople which the merchant ships brought to her with prodigality. All of these chairs are of the square construction that endures, and all have baluster legs but of different styles of turning. All are understayed with honest stretchers, but one has the front stretcher close to the floor, indicating a little earlier mode. The colonnade of arches forming the back is nearer its Italian origin where a column supports the arch rather than a bulbous spindle.

One more feature to note on these chairs, that is common to both late Tudor and early Jacobean styles, is the decoration of split spindles or pendants applied to a flat surface. This decoration is a favourite for wood panelling, for chests of drawers and all large pieces about the middle of the century.

We have but to call to mind the costume of Henrietta Maria, the queen of Charles I, to realise why these armless chairs were the most popular of the time; the voluminous skirts of the ladies of the court —whom others imitated—could not have been squeezed into an arm chair with courtly grace.

The sort of room in which this furniture was set—
how happy we of to-day would be to have their panelling! Occasionally an entire room is taken from
some old English home and set up in one of our
American dwellings, such as the rooms now owned
by Mr. Frederick Pratt and Mr. W. R. Hearst. And
thus we know what beauty surrounded the English
family three hundred years ago. Panelling in
squares covered the walls from floor to ceiling or to
a high level, above which hung tapestries or embroid-
eries. And as the architect of the house composed
the panelling it was drawn with such skill as to miss
either hap-hazard or monotony.

The linen-fold panel of Gothic and early Tudor
popularity was no longer repeated. The true
Jacobean panel is small and square with carving on
the pilasters and cornice in rooms of elegance. To
this day no more home-like way of treating the walls
of large rooms has been devised than this wood
panelling, which gives a sense of seclusion and of
richness that is never so well imparted except by the
use of tapestry—and the combination of the two
nearly approaches perfection.

Jacobean styles, so-called, extend through the
greater part of the century, but each succeeding
Stuart marked his special progress on them. The
styles of the first kings, James I and his son Charles I,
lifted the family movables from heaviness to com-
parative lightness, and grew away from the Renais-

Plate X—OAK CHEST OF DRAWERS

An interesting example of the Jacobean use of decorative mouldings

Plate XI—EARLY JACOBEAN CABINET

Carved and put together with wooden pegs. A guilloche carving ornaments each panel

sance in truly original ways.   On this fact rests much of its interest.   The other great fact for us is that these years of the first Stuart kings were the years of the first American colonisation.

# CHAPTER II

## JACOBEAN STYLES TO CHARLES II

BRUTALLY natural we may call the earlier characters in English history, but attached to the Stuart name there is always poetic romance. And without romance what would our lives be! So when we sit in our loved library or dining-room at home, embellished by a few bits of furniture such as the Stuarts lived among, those bits are like consolidated stories, things to dream about in the hours of ease.

James I and his son Charles cared about things they lived with, and cared, too, about giving them as much as possible a certain lightness of effect, in revolt from Tudor bulk. Perhaps the necessity for surpassing strength was waning. Men no longer wore tons of armour, furniture in the seventeenth century no longer journeyed from castle to castle. Inigo Jones was at work also, with his marvellous talent at classical architecture, setting a standard of cheerful elegance in design that lightened the Tudor magnificence.

When James I began to rule in 1603, Inigo Jones, a lightsome young man of thirty, was employed by

the King as a composer of masques.    After develop-
ing his architect's talent he produced the palace at
Whitehall, Hatfield House and other residences.
His also was the invention that threw over the steps
to the Thames the noble water-gate, York Stairs,
that stands there now, a record of the merry days
when ladies and cavaliers, all gay as flowers, crossed
the greensward, filed under this richly carved arch,
and were handed into elegantly equipped barges on
the river.

While things of an artistic sort were progressing
in England, other events closely concerning us in
America were also active.    The entire century runs
two parallel lines of history, one that of the gaiety
of the house in power, the other that of the struggle
of the people divided into religious sects.    While
" 'twas merry in the Hall, when beards wagged all,"
persecution was rife among religionists, and the
Puritans were finding it hard to stay in their own
loved land.

Thus came the sufferers to America to plant new
homes; and thus coming, brought with them such
furniture as was in vogue at the time of migrating.
And so it happens that our earliest bits of furniture,
chairs that supported grim Pilgrim fathers, tables
which were set out by provident Puritan mothers and
maids, are Jacobean in mode.    The chair of Elder
Brewster which has asylum in Hartford, Conn., is a
fine example of the heavy turned work of the day,

and numerous oak chairs show the strap-work and other low-relief carving so well known in early Jacobean pieces.

One especial class of chair (Plate 12) when found in England is called for one of its shires, Yorkshire, but when drawn from New England hiding places, we name it a wainscote chair. The design of the back easily gives reason for the name, for it is formed from a bit of panelling similar to that in vogue for walls. Stolid and strong are these chairs, square-built and stayed with four strong stretchers, usually near the floor.

The collector considers the charm irresistibly increased when the front stretcher is well worn with the friction of many feet, the resting feet of a long procession that has walked down the centuries. Even better is the smoothness of the chair-arms which comes by contact with the human hand, that restless member with a habit of idly rubbing an inviting surface. Like all makers of chairs, the ancient cabinet-maker left back-legs in utilitarian simplicity, while he limited variety to the front-legs. In this type of chair, turning gave the usual ornamentation. This baluster effect had many varieties, but all united in finishing with a square block at the bottom and where the seat-frame met the leg, or where the front stretcher crossed, if it was placed high.

The ornamentation of the back was done with the light spirit that distinguished early Jacobean styles

Plate XII—OAK CHAIRS
Called both Wainscote and Yorkshire chairs

Plate XIII—SPIRAL TURNED CHAIR, CHARACTERISTIC OF FIRST HALF
OF CENTURY

from the preceding Italian models, yet without the elegance that appeared later in the century. These chairs undoubtedly have charm and interest, but as works of art they are not comparable to those which preceded, nor to those which followed. They were, however, distinctly English, and as such, command interest.

A close study of the motifs used by the wood-carver shows all the favourite lines, the guilloche, that ever interesting play upon circles, the S curve in pairs, the rounded arch, the half-circle, the rose and the tulip. Cushions were a part of the chair's equipment. The tired ladies of the seventeenth century were not asked to recuperate on a thick oak plank un-softened by padding. Loose cushions of velvet and of embroidery were usual, for this was an age when handsome fabrics were made all over Europe, and freely used in flashing blue and ruby red against the oak.

Nearly allied to the wainscote chair, yet infinitely more refined, is the chair of spiral parts, with back and seat upholstered. Without arms it was favoured by ladies of voluminous petticoats who pattered about the thrones of James I and Charles I. With arms it is sometimes called Cromwellian, suggesting that the doughty Dictator ruled therefrom. But the austerity of the wainscote chair seems more fitting to his resolute manner.

This turned chair with its padded back and seat,

so often dignifies our modern interiors that it is worth
our while to know about it. While the wainscote
chair belonged more especially to cottage furniture
which was made all over England according to varying local taste, this chair was more or less of an
aristocrat, and furnished the halls of wealth. Its
origin is Italian. France used it freely, but she too
got her first model from the Italians. In the time
these chairs prevailed, England outside of London
was scant of luxury. The homes of all but the
wealthiest were short of the comforts that ameliorate
the jolt of life's car in these our modern days.

But the whole country was sprinkled with inns and
taverns wherein were gathered such luxuries as the
times afforded, and thither went the man of the
family, bored by the too rigid manner of the home.
Those who travelled, too, in the saddle or by lumber-
ing coach, fell happily into the warm embrace of the
chairs at the hospitable inn at each stop on the jour-
ney. The post-road made the string, the inns the
pearls, and in this way the surface of England was
covered with a net for the delectation of the restless.
But old-time descriptions of the highways, their ruts
and sloughs, their highwaymen even, show how
laborious were the journeyings and how more than
glad were travellers to alight.

Ben Jonson declared a tavern chair to be the
throne of human felicity. Thus he spoke praise, not
only of the inn but of such furniture as pleases us in

these days.  If, therefore, any husband of to-day
rebel against the stiffness of backs, or weakness
of legs, of the antique chairs at home, let him be
reminded of Jonson's opinion on these same
chairs.

The chair with spiral legs and other members runs
through the larger half of the century, and has sig-
nificant variations.  One shown on Plate 13 has a
female head on the uprights of the arms, which represents Mary of Modena.  The figure is given at
full length in a model that our furniture manufacturers have many times repeated.

While baluster legs for chairs and other furniture
were a product of the reign of the first James, we
may set down the more elegant spiral twist as an evidence of a better developed taste for which a few
leaders were responsible.  Such a man as Inigo
Jones must have influenced widely the public taste
in all liberal arts.  Although his examples were set
in the larger art of architecture, the crowd swagger-
ing about the Banqueting Hall, which still excites
our delight at Whitehall, must have been inspired
to introduce a daintier style at home.

It was in 1625 that Charles I succeeded his father,
and soon after invited Van Dyck to be of those who
surrounded the royal person.  It sometimes seems to
the art-seeking tourist, that Charles' patronage of art
had as motive the production of an infinity of portraits of his own much-frizzed, much-dressed self.

But apart from painting portraits of the King, which the model made a bit pathetic, through the attempt to associate majesty with preciosity, Van Dyck had a large part in improving England's taste. Another name is that of Sir Francis Crane, he who helped his royal master with the noble art of tapestry-making at the Mortlake Works.

To continue with the use of the spiral leg—as its modern use creates interest in the subject—it is found as the support on those most enticing of tables, the gate-leg. Not that all gate-leg tables are thus made. Alas no, economy travels heavily in all ages, so the less expensive baluster turning prevailed. But the spiral is the favourite and gives great value to the old tables. Rarely indeed are they to be found at bargains since we in America have taken to collecting Jacobean furnishings.

Gate-leg tables are labelled with the name of Cromwell by those liking to fix a date by attaching to it a ruler. Without doubt, the great Commoner leaned his weary elbows on such a table when things went wrong, or curved a smiling lip above it—if he could smile—when the table was weighted with savoury Puritan viands. But for many years before Cromwell, English homes had found the gate-leg table a mobile and convenient replacer of the massive refectory tables of Tudor or Roman inspiration.

In large size these tables set a feast for the family, in smaller drawing they held the evening light; or,

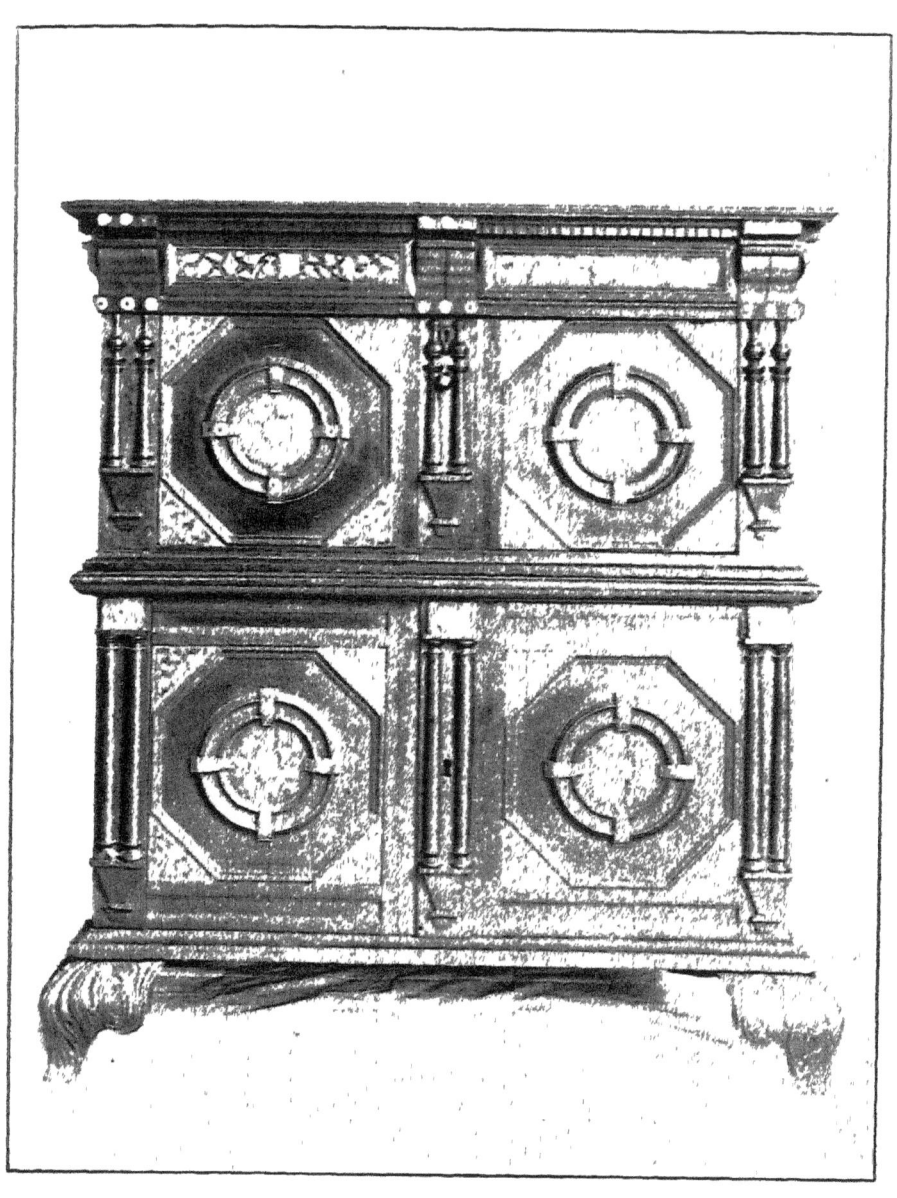

Plate XIV—OAK CABINET, DATED 1653

Decorated with split spindles, and with inlay mother-of-pearl, ivory and ebony.
The legs show tendencies not developed until the next century
under Queen Anne

Plate XV—OAK GATE-LEG DINING TABLE

With oval top and rarely proportioned spiral legs  A drawer distinguishes the piece

smaller yet, they assisted the house-mother at her sewing. The wonder is not that we of to-day find them invaluable, but that mankind ever let them go out of fashion. Collect them if you have the purse, but if you must buy a modern copy, remember that mahogany was not in use for furniture in England until the century after, for modern manufacturers flout chronology and produce gate-leg tables in the wood of which the originals were never made. They even lacquer them, in defiance of history.

Since the fashion is for old tables in the dining-room, these Jacobean gate-leg tables are found practical as well as beautiful. The large size, about four and a half feet wide by six feet long, accommodates a moderate family and presents none of the inconveniences that make certain antiques mere objects of art or curios. I must confess to a thrill of delight when sitting at such an old oak board set out with old lace and silver, not only for its obvious beauty, but by the thought of the groups who have gathered there through three hundred years, groups of varying customs, varying habits of thought, varying fashions in dress, yet human like ourselves, and prone to make of the dining-table a circle of joy.

The inlaid cabinet on Plate 11 is an aristocrat. Though it is dated 1653 it exhibits the split spindles of earlier years, and these are executed with such nice feeling that they accord well with the Italian look of the piece. In truth, its principal decoration

is Italian, an elaborate use of inlay in mother of
pearl, ivory and ebony. Its feet, too, are entirely
un-English, yet it remains a Jacobean piece of English make. The influences always at work in England left their mark on the development of English
styles. Always and always a monarch was marry-
ing a foreign wife, or importing a court painter or
architect, and these folk naturally brought with them
the fashions of their own countries. It seemed as
though the English knew that native art was not a
flower of the first order of beauty and so were modest
about it, and ever willing to adopt the art of other
countries.

It is the custom of the inexact to include in Jacobean furniture all the styles of the seventeenth century up to the time of William and Mary, and this
gives to such loose classification an extraordinary
variety. Furniture does not die with a monarch, nor
do new designs start up in a night; goods last after
the master has gone, and the new master uses the old
style until a later one has been evolved. James died
and Charles I took his place in the year 1625, but the
lightening and elaborating of furniture came not all
at once, and depended as much on mechanical invention and the use of new woods as on the rise and fall
of monarchs.

And yet, as the first man to be pleased was the
king, and as the king in Charles' case had a lighter
nature than his forerunners and had moreover a Con-

tinental encouraging of that lightness, we fancy we see an evidence of gaiety, of jocundity, in the furniture of his day. He was a king who intended to take all the privileges of his state, and one of these was to surround himself with beauty of the type that brought no reminders of hard living nor serious thinking, no hint of grim Puritan asceticism.

So the oak of England which had supplied austerity was now carved into shapes hitherto unknown. Typical of the results of elaborate oak carving are the chairs in Plate 17. The arm-chair is a typical example of a chair of the middle years of the century, and later. Here the square construction of the chair is not altered from Tudor days, but note how every part has been lightened, until an elegance and beauty have been attained which make it worthy of the finest rooms of any time. The carver when given free rein has left little of the chair untouched. Legs, stretchers and uprights, are all made with a well proportioned spiral, and at each square of joining a rosette is carved.

Here also is seen an innovation in the ornamental stretcher across the front which, instead of being near the ground, is raised to a height out of reach of a ruthless boot which might mar its elaboration. This stretcher shows the use of the long curving palm in place of the classic acanthus, and also introduces the fat little cherubs which French designers affected.

Other points to notice are the very open back, composed of spirals and three rows of carving. It was at this time that pierced carving came into vogue, so far surpassing in beauty the wainscote backs.

The incising of the seat-frame is another peculiarity of the middle of the century. Perhaps the most interesting matter of all is the caning. Wooden seats were the only ones hitherto; although cushions had been used to soften them, they lacked at best the reciprocal quality that we call "giving." Springs were far in the future, but a luxury-loving aristocracy seized at once upon this amelioration.

There is more or less quibbling upon the subject of caning, as to the date of its introduction. No one can fix it exactly, which robs the enthusiast of the pleasure of announcing with oracular precision, that his chair is of certain year because of its caning. The middle of the century saw it, the first part did not, but it lasted through varying styles of furniture, and is lasting still.

Its origin is undoubtedly Eastern, for the tenacious splints from which it is woven are from warmer climes than England's. And that brings us again to one of those little facts in history of which our household gods are ever reminding us, the trade that united India with Portugal, Portugal with Flanders, and the Flemish with England.

The small chair in the Plate is, to the careless eye, a little sister to the larger, but the wise observer notes at once the substitution of the S curve heavy in carv-

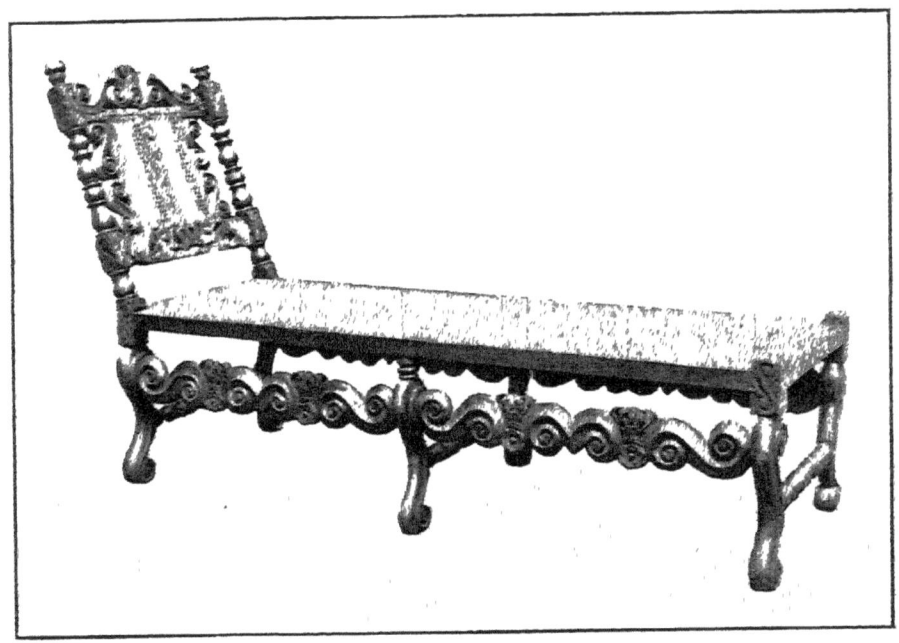

Plate XVI—OAK DAY BEDS
Carved after manner in vogue in second half of XVII Century

Plate XVII—STUART CHAIRS

Of lightened construction, open carving and incised seat frame

ing for the more elaborate pierced palm. Also the
cane panels in the back, and the very decided change
in the shape of the front legs. The heavy S curves
are the same which later on gain in thickness and
evolve into the ogee curve seen later, and which is
often mistakenly ascribed to William and Mary, although originating earlier and receives the name of
James II. Arbitrary names are hard to make consistently exact; dates are hard to place on every piece,
but is it not enough to know within a very few years
the time of making of one's valuable antiques?

To finish the scrutiny of the smaller chair, note the
curve of the front legs, the first attempt at deserting
the straight perpendicular line of construction. This
is the beginning of an insidious French influence
which prevailed throughout the last third of the century. It beautified, of course, as the gift of France
to the world is the *luxe* of the eye, but from the time
of its introduction dates the end of the furniture
which was of solely English invention.

So comes the end of this early Jacobean mode, in
its best time of flowering when it was drowned in a
flood of foreign influence. It was in the styles prevailing through the reigns of the first two Stuarts
and of Cromwell, that England expressed only her-
self in her furniture. It is this which makes the
periods rich with originality and of peculiar interest.
When the Jacobean styles began Shakespeare was
living those sad years whose disillusion produced his

later plays, and Jacobean styles were at their height at the Restoration when Charles II played the part of king for his royal pleasure.

# CHAPTER III

## THE MIDDLE OF THE CENTURY

### END OF THE PURE JACOBEAN

TWO matters influenced greatly the furniture makers of the middle of the seventeenth century. And these had less to do with kings and courts than with humble folk. One was the invention of a saw, the kind of a saw that would divide a plank into as many thin sheets of wood as were desired. Naturally, those who looked upon these thin sheets imagined new ways of using them for the embellishment of furniture.

Heavy carving had been almost the only ornament when inch-thick planks were the usual material. Now, a wondrous field of possibilities lay before the ambitious in the way of inlay and veneer. Possibly André Boulle in France gave the inspiration, but even so the English inlay is a matter all by itself. From the invention of that saw arose a style of decoration that developed from such simplicity as the rare and occasional flower seen on early Jacobean panels, to the exquisite elaboration known as the seaweed pattern, and other masses of curving filaments, which found highest perfection in the last quarter of the century.

The cabinets on Plates 18 and 19 illustrate the almost unbelievable fineness of the work. In the larger cabinet the inlay is drawn with a free hand and is less characteristic of English design than the other, excepting the naïveté of the birds and trees, and the central panel wherein a gaily caparisoned youth strides a horse held by an infinitesimal blackamoor—a bit of the East's submission thus noted.

Wherever a plain surface was found, the new ornament seized it. Cabinets and chests of drawers offered the best opportunities, but next to them were tables. The tops gave a fine field—although there is always a lack of unity of feeling between a table maker and a table user. The one thinks the table should be left inviolably empty, the other regards it as a rest for books and bibelots. But there is also the drawer of the table and its apron, so upon these the inlay designs were put in all their dainty beauty of design.

This class of work must not be in any way confused with the Dutch inlay of a later epoch and which is imitated to-day ad nauseam. If you have naught else to guide you in knowing the old English from modern Dutch, there are the shapes of the pieces on which the inlay is put, besides the pattern of the work.

The second matter which made a change in the general aspect of furniture in the second half of the seventeenth century was the use of walnut wood in

Plate XVIII—MARQUETRY CABINET ABOUT 1700
Showing Dutch Indian influence in its design and ornament

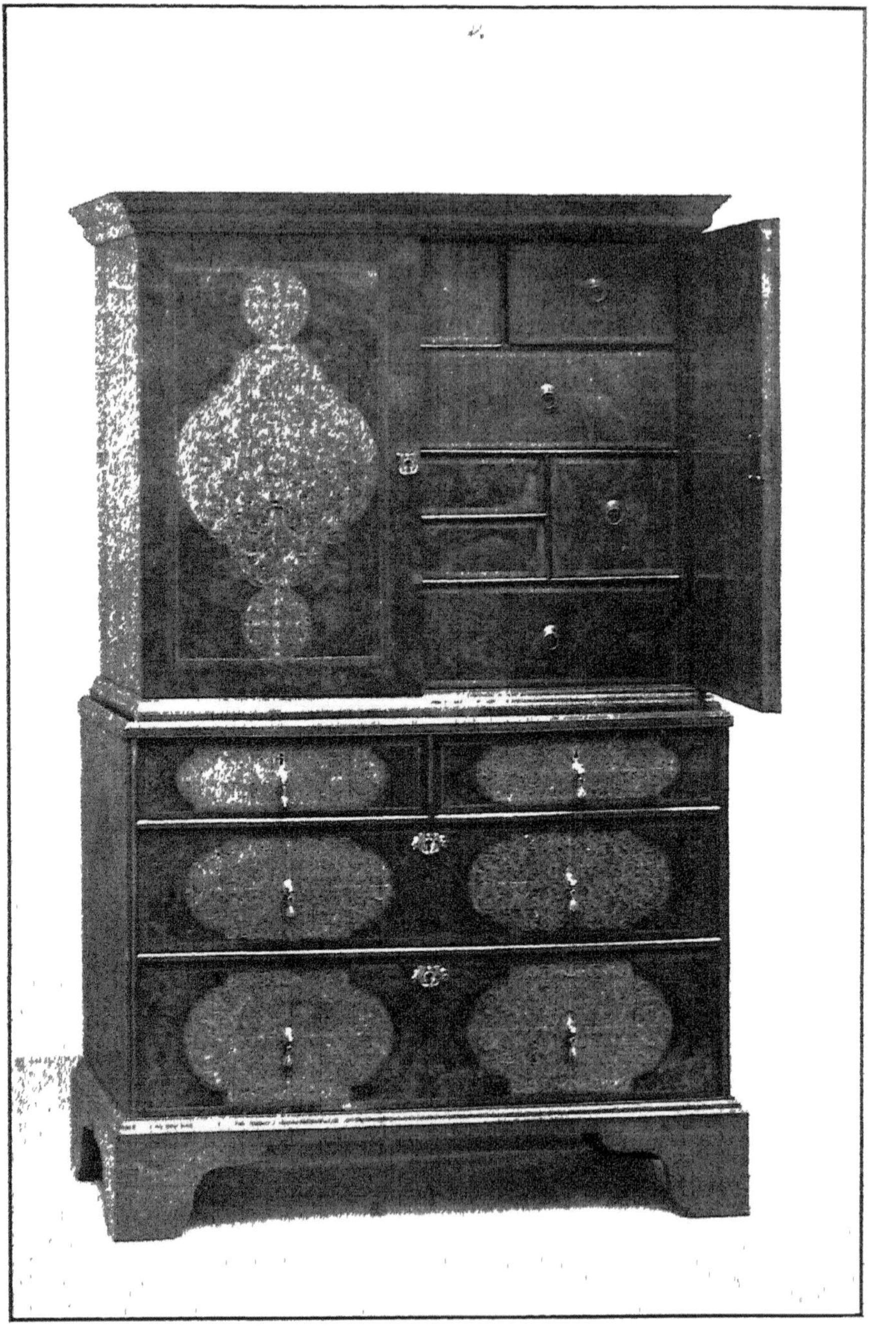

**Plate XIX—WALNUT CABINET**

With veneer and inlay of seaweed pattern showing the extreme skill of cabinet
workers in the second half of the XVII century.
Drop handles are noticeable

place of oak. It is a pretty bit of history, that of the rich-toned walnut. As far back as Elizabeth's day furniture of that wood was imported from Italy in all its beauty of design, colour and finish. The wise queen ordered trees brought from Italy and forests planted, that England might have a supply of the admired wood. She did not live to see the trees of use, but in the century following hers, it came suddenly into vogue. Imagine the delight of those who had been working in the more obdurate oak, to feel this finer, softer wood under the tool.

Putting together the invention of the saw which could slice wood as thin as paper as well as fret it into sea-weed, and the adoption of walnut wood, still another type of beauty in furniture was produced, that of the plain large-panelled scheme. By cunning skill panels of walnut veneer were produced where the grain of the wood supplied the design. Add to this the wonderful finish of the cabinet-maker, and the piece had the beauty of bronze and the simplicity of classicism. But no picture can give adequate idea of the beauty of the old burr walnut. Its bronze surface of innumerable tones, all polished by generations of caressing hands and never by varnish, must be seen and touched to be appreciated. The patine of time is heightened by the patine of affection, and both together make of the plain walnut furniture a thing of appealing beauty to those who love restraint in ornament.

A word about this thing we call patine. It began in these old pieces with the original finish of the old maker, who, having done all of the work himself, was tenderly careful of results. This early necromancer played on the wood of his precious meuble with soothing oil, with tonic of turpentine and with protective wax. With the oil he fed the open pores of the wood, until all were filled against the attack of less judicious nutriment, then with pungent turpentine and fragrant honest wax, he rubbed patiently the surfaces. No varnish, as he valued his art. Varnish as we know it now was not in his laboratory. It was not needed when every man was lavish of the labour of his hand.

Thus was begun the patine for which we collectors cry to-day. But the assistance of the housewife was a necessary adjunct, for never through all the centuries must she do other than rub with oil and wax the fine old oak and walnut. I have seen the work of centuries destroyed by a modern vandal with a can of varnish.

The lawns of England are made by centuries of unremitting care. The patine on old English furniture is brought about by the same virtue. If there be any who do not value the rare old finish, then for his household wares the manufacturers provide a vat of varnish into which whole sets of chairs are dipped to avoid even the labour of brushing on a coat of the shiny stuff.

Roundhead and Cavalier each had to be suited with furniture, so the varying styles, the elaborate and the plain, met all requirements. In the midst of it all reigned Charles, the second of the Stuart kings, fostering art with his wondrous assistant Van Dyck, and making a thousand mistakes in the art of government, yet ever standing a romantic figure. We feel an interest in all that concerned his life as a man, feeling more pity than indignation at his futile descent upon Parliament to pluck therefrom the five members who offended him. And who does not, when in London, glance at his high-bred marble effigy at Whitehall with a secret sympathy for his miserable end? We all love a gentleman, and time has nothing to do with effacing that. The elegance Charles I introduced into his time delights us now, and we thrill at the thought of owning any of the fine accessories with which he or his nobles surrounded themselves.

After Charles came the Commonwealth. Republican as we are, we feel an unaccountable revolt against any suggestion of Cromwell's taste in life's elegant accessories. He was the great Commoner, and as such has no skill at dictating fashions for aristocrats. So we accord to him a leather-covered chair with spiral turned frame, and a gate-leg table, feeling he should be grateful for the award, as even these things were not of his own invention.

Of the two great divisions, the Cavaliers and the

Roundheads, the aristocratic party fell into subjection. All that was austere came to the fore, and all that had the charm of gaiety and mirth, elegance and extravagance, was disapproved by those in power. Cromwell's personality did not inspire the makers of pretty kickshaws for my lady's boudoir, nor luxuries for my lord's hall. So nothing was to be done by the cabinet-makers but to repeat the previous styles.

The asceticism of the Puritan inspired no art in the few years of Roundhead rule, but there is no telling what might have happened had Cromwell stayed several decades in power. At the end he took most kindly to living in the royal palace of Hampton Court. The quick assumption of elegance of the beggar on horseback is proverbial. After Napoleon had forgotten his origin, no king was more acquisitive than he in the matter of thrones and palaces, nor more insistent in the matter of royal pomp. But "Old Noll" did not live to rule like a prince of the blood, nor to develop a style of luxurious living that left a mark on the liberal arts.

The development of walnut furniture went imperceptibly on, with oak still much in use, when all at once a new fact in history gave a new excuse for changes in the mode. The Cromwells passed and the people of England took back the House of Stuart, and did it with such enthusiasm that even the furniture reflected it at once. But it is just this reflection of events in the art of a period that gives undying interest to old styles, and especially to those ancient pieces that are left from the hands which made them and those who first used them in palace or cottage.

Back, then, came the old delight in royally born royalty, in being governed by a king and not by a commoner. With open arms the king was welcomed, and Cavalier families that had been in sad plight, blotted out by confiscation and disapproval, sprang lightly back to their former places. This was the time of the Restoration, that time when England adopted the rottenness of the Continent to stimulate whatever of vice lay in the Briton, forgetting to take with it the fundamental good. But the naughty game was one so prettily played that we never tire of its recounting. And as it produced so many changes in house furnishings, it must be considered.

It was in 1660 that Charles II was called to smile from the throne on a pleased public. It was about that time that a queen was chosen for him, Catherine of Braganza, who brought with her, very naturally, some goods of her own.

The styles in England at this time were especially England's, he native effort fred from copying Italy's Renaissance. But on this fell a sudden avalanche of new ideas greatly at variance with her methods, and from now on the styles of England took inspiration from the styles of the Continent, and have ever since continued the game.

But let this sink into the consciousness: each

style adopted takes on the strong characteristics of the country adopting them.    If to originate a decorative style was not the natural impulse of Britain, it was her talent to alter that style in a way that expressed her characteristics.    In the time of Charles II she had a love for the light side of life, coupled with prodigality and elegance, and this can be read to-day in the relics of those times.

Catherine the Queen brought no children to inherit the throne—the Duke of York being accused of having selected purposefully a barren mate for his brother—but she brought Bombay as a dower.    So, with her Portuguese furniture and her Eastern designs, her gifts turned the heads of artists and artisans.    In England are found those chairs for which we go to Portugal, yet they were made in England in the seventeenth century, the high-back straight chair covered with carved leather in both back and seat, put on with a prodigality of big nails, and having bronze spikes as a finish to the uprights of the back. The fluted foot came then, a sort of compromise between a claw and scroll, and known in our land as a Spanish foot, and used until the end of the seventeenth century.    It is found on much furniture of early Colonial times prior to Anne's day.

But perhaps the first change in Charles' reign was seen on the chairs of pierced carving of palm and S curve and cherub, with caned seats or backs.    The carving on these chairs at once took as its popular

device the crown, the crown which had been hidden
out of sight in the years of the Commonwealth. As
if to show the wealth of affection with which it was
welcomed, it was repeated as many as five conspicu-
ous times on one chair. With what complacence
must Charles have looked upon this gentle flattery!

For the Queen's satisfaction there were matters
from the Near East in the way of ivory and ebony
inlay, carved ebony, introductions of small black be-
ings into designs, always in obvious subjection to
white masters. But these were exotics of a sort
that English taste preferred to import rather than
manufacture. Ladies who took to embroidering affected the Bombay designs and colours.

Charles II had been reigning but six years when
the Great Fire swept away uncountable treasures in
the way of furniture. To be sure, there was all the
rest of England. But at that time London was prac-
tically all of elegant England. Country gentlemen
had estates and big houses, but owing to the impos-
sibility of transportation on the always miry, rutted
roads, they went without the luxuries of town life.
So, with the Great Fire of London perished so much
of old oak and walnut furniture as to make collectors
weep who turn their thoughts thereon.

But as the phœnix rises unabashed from the
flames, so rose the inspirations of Sir Christopher
Wren, Grinling Gibbons, and of minor artists and
artisans. Wren rebuilt the fallen monuments, giving

to the world his great St. Paul's, and a pattern of
church steeple that climbs high in American settle-
ments as well as all through London; and he lesser
workers gave men new patterns in beds and chairs
for repose, and in tables for comforting viands, for
games, or for the gossip which was a deep game of
the day.

# CHAPTER IV

## CAROLEAN STYLES OR THE RESTORATION

### CHARLES II, 1660 TO 1685

IF it was to the Queen of Charles II that the Carolean period of furniture owed its Portuguese strain and the evidence of strange things from the East, it was from a woman of quite another sort that the predominating influence came. French styles were the vogue at court, not because the Queen, poor dull woman, wished it, but because Louise de Querouailles was the strong influence, and with her advent came follies and fashions enough to please the light side of one of the lightest of monarchs. France, in the person of Louis XIV, felt that England would bear watching while a Stuart strutted and flirted, oppressed and vacillated. And the Fren·h ways of those days being directed by such craft as that of the astute Cardinal Mazarin, a woman was sent from France to charm the King and stay closer beside the throne than any man could bide.

Charles created the light and lovely Louise the Duchess of Portsmouth and the mother of the little Duke of Richmond; and, that so much of extravagant beauty might be royally housed, he spent much

time and more money in fitting her apartments at
Whitehall.    Three times were they demolished at
her whim, the extravagant fittings failing to suit her
insatiable caprice.

Such procedure was hotly stimulating to artists
and artisans.    In the first attempt they sought to
produce their best, but seeing it displease, they were
lashed on to more and yet more subtle effort until at
last the pretty lady of too much power had forced
the production of elegant new styles which smacked
of her native France.    Thus went by the board the
efforts of English styles to remain English, and thus
began that long habit of keeping an eye on French
designs.

We think of Charles II as a figure-head of romance, because the rosy mist of poetic fancy clings
to the members of the Stuart family from Mary of
Scots down to—but not including—that Duke of
York who minced about the throne of Charles II
with his soul concentrated on securing from his
brother his own personal advancement.

The horrors of Charles' reign, the Bloody As-
sizes, the Monmouth incident, his neglect to recognise the seriousness of his responsibilities, all these
things are lost in the elegant frivolity of the life led
at his court.    Cares, ennuis, tragedies, were flicked
aside by white hands thrust from brocades and lace,
and a merry measure was the antidote for soul-sick-
ness.

;o made music or danced to it, those who
rh,      ʜe naughtier the better) and sang their
verses, th,·se who led at toasts and feasting, those
who wore the richest dress, were the persons of im-
portance under the patronage of Charles II, in the
time of the Restoration.

Nell Gwynn, she of the quick smile and quick tear,
and vulnerable heart, was of the King's favour to the
extent of honouring him with the little Duke of St.
Albans; and on her Charles lavished accessories of
elegant living similar to those he bestowed on
Louise de Querouailles. The bewitching actress
lived her quickly changing moods among the furniture that now graces our modern rooms here on this
side of the water.

We were not importing many of those elegances
in 1664.   That was the date when Charles' brother
James, Duke of York, left the luxurious court at
London and came to give royal dignity to the little
American town of New Amsterdam on the day when
its Dutch dominion ended and the city was re-
christened New York.

While considering the fascinating women of the
court, Hortensia Mancini, for whom beautiful furnishings were made, must stand as the most al-
luring of them all because she ever eludes the critic
or dissector. Somewhat of her uncle Cardinal
Mazarin was in her astute secretiveness, but a baf-
fling quality all her own made her proof against sur-

rendering her soul to any man's probing or
man's charm.  So rich she was that money co...
tempt; so clever, with Italian wit added to ...
culture, that none could surpass her in repa...
discourse; so full of mystery was her da...
piquant beauty that all might envy her—yet ...
sionately unhappy, that none would wish to ex...
with her.

Add to the list of women Barbara Palmer, D...-
ess of Cleveland, who represented a heavy v...
ousness and a prolific motherhood for the Ki...,
we see the women favoured by the King's a...
and for whom the beautiful furnishings of t...
were produced.

Though Charles II had no royal factories ...
Louis XIV was conducting in France, plenty ...
objects of art were yielded by the workers.  ...
astonishing aberration of taste, silver furniture...
a vogue at this time, the King considering ...
vourite worthy of such extravagance.  It must have
been ugly by its inappropriateness, however pretty
was the woman it served.

Louise de Querouailles had hers set in a room
lined all with mirror glass, which at that time was an
expensive novelty.  But it pleased the King to wan-
der into the apartment of his favourite satellite and
see the lovely image of the Duchess of Portsmouth
sitting among her silver movables, reflected so many
times in the walls that the world seemed peopled only

with adorable women. Nell Gwynn also had her mirror room.

It was the Duke of Buckingham who made the mirror-lined room possible by establishing a factory for mirrors. Previous to this time they were exceeding rare in England. Now a leaf was taken from Italy's books and mirrors were made at home, with bevelled edges, and also with bright blue glass framing, inside the wooden frame.

Grinling Gibbons was at work on his carvings and inventions, and we have record of him as a decorator in a letter in which he tells his lady client: "I holp all things will please you." It was the year after the Great Fire, 1667, that Gibbons began to make a feature of the garlands and swags of flowers and fruit, carved with excessive exuberance, that are associated with his name and that of Queen Anne in decoration. To gain his effects he used the fine soft limewood as yielding to his tool almost like a plastic stuff.

In social England Bath played an important part, and thither went for new scenes the merry gossiping crowd for their routs and aristocratic carousing. This was the time of the sedan-chair, of the dropped note, the flirted handkerchief, the raised eyebrow and the quick eye-flash, all full of poignant meanings of their own. Life was a pretty game, insistently a pretty one, and following the mode, its accessories were pretty. At Bath the same elegant crowd played as in London, transferred by shockingly primitive coaches over outrageously rutted roads. The wonder is they ever cared to undertake such hardships as those imposed on travellers in England in the seventeenth century. But at Bath we see them, at the famous spas, with Nell Gwynn, wayward and ardent, charming the men, slighted by the women.

To be specific about the furniture styles of the times is satisfactory to the student, to the desired end that old pieces may be known from imitation, and that good adaptations may be distinguished from bad. In general it may be said that lightness continued to be the ideal in construction, particularly in chairs and tables, and that carvings grew ever finer in workmanship. Chair backs also grew narrower and higher. Caning was retained, but seats were covered with a squab cushion, or upholstered. A minute examination of the chairs on Plate 21 leads to the detection of certain characteristics. This Plate shows a particularly good example of the chairs as they depart from the fashion which prevailed immediately before the Fire, and as they merged into the style of William and Mary.

These chairs have details in common with chairs that preceded them, but as a whole, they are entirely different. They do not tell the same story, convey the same message, as the chairs of Charles I, for example. And that shows the subtle power of fur-

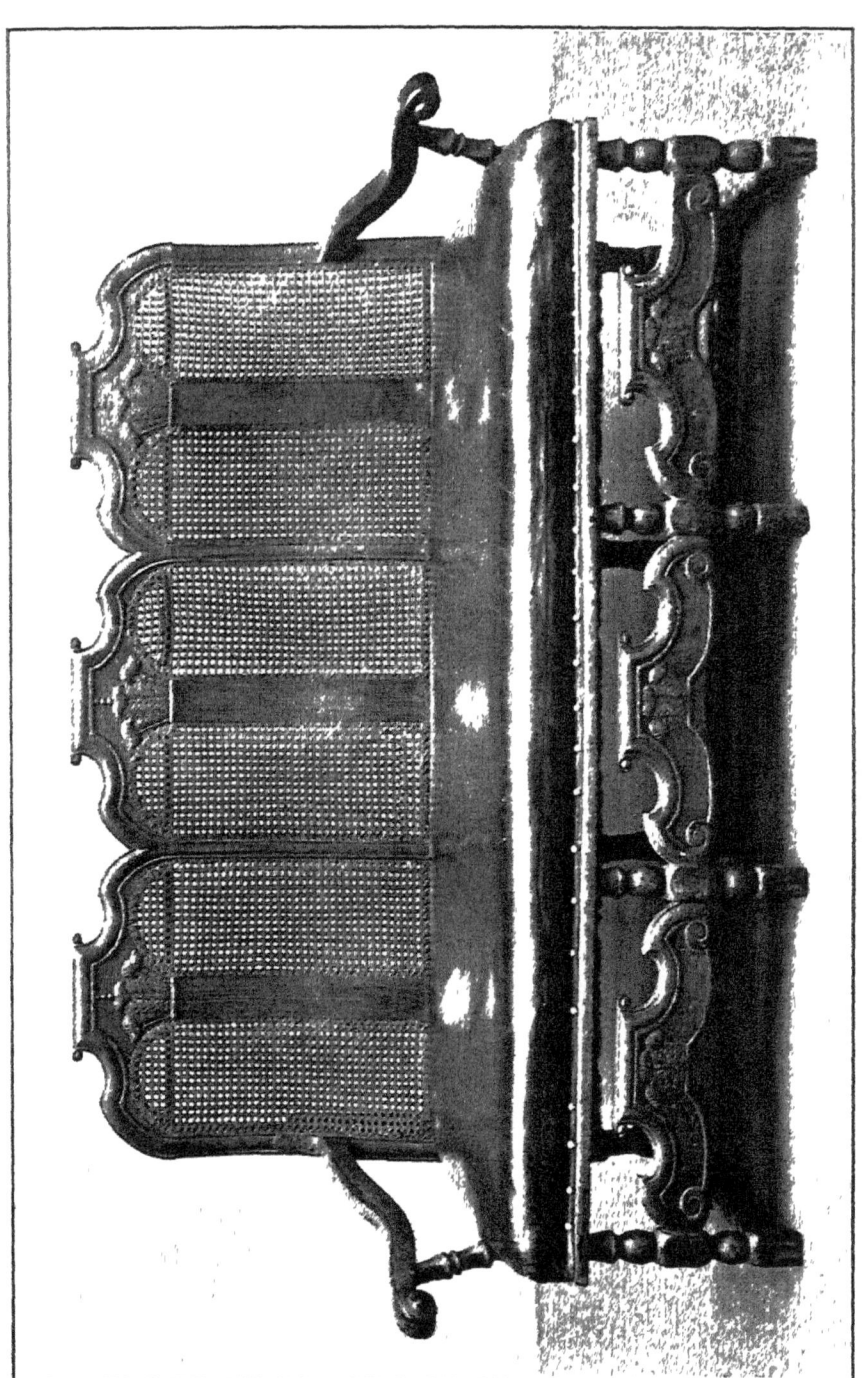

Plate XX—STUART SETTEE WITH CARVING. SECOND HALF OF XVII CENTURY

Plate XXI—CHARLES II CHAIRS OF VARYING STYLES IN CARVING

niture to express the spirit of the times in which it was made. "Feeling" is a word for the serious collector. Ability to read feeling amounts almost to a talent, and is certainly an instinct. Those who possess it know without recourse to detail where to place a piece of furniture never encountered before, and this even though it be one of those erratic pieces that appear in all periods. The feeling, then, of these chairs is French, but a transplanted French, growing under alien influence.

Descending upon details, the shape of the legs is so much at variance with those of the preceding fashion that they seem to alter the scheme of construction. By means of the change from a straight line to a curve the chair loses in honesty and in balance while growing in elegance.

Another point to notice is the change in the arrangement of stretchers, also the lifting from the floor of the elaborate front stretcher which is made to match the ornamental top of the chair back. The seat-frame retains the incising of the former fashion, and the square blocks at points of intersection carry the familiar carved rosette. The backs have strong points of interest. The radical change is in the uprights, which, instead of being wide, flat carvings of leafage, are gracefully designed posts. A long step in the way of beauty was made when this style of back was adopted, a treatment which developed later in the century into the exquisite carved backs, which even exceeded the French in graceful invention. An examination of the chairs of 1685 will show the perfection of the style which was begun by Charles II, adopted by James II and further developed under William and Mary.

To continue the lesson of the chairs, it was here that the old flat S curve began to alter into the richer, more robust C curve. The leg of chairs carved in C scrolls follows the shape of the curves, and furniture of this pattern has exceeding charm, especially when the front stretcher has been treated by an inspired hand. Much sought are the chairs and sofas of this period, and when covered with needle-point are keenly valued for use in the superb living-room which in modern homes often takes place of the drawing-room.

Happy indeed is the collector who can find such an old English sofa as that in the Metropolitan Museum on Plate 22. It is entirely characteristic, and shows not only the interesting fashion in carving, but the large advance in upholstering. Such comfortable work was unknown before the reign of Charles II. If we have curiosity as to the appearance of the gentlefolk who used such furniture, the embroidered cover of this piece shows lovely woman in her hours of ease, and mankind hovering near with a wish to please. But this very embroidery shows how difficult a matter it was for the English to draw with true hand and free, a purely decorative motive; for,

Plate XXII—WALNUT SOFA

Carved in C curves, time of James II covered with petit point embroidery

Plate XXIII—GILT MIRROR, TIME OF CHARLES II
When mirrors were freely made in England

outside the figures of the medallions, the whole thing is meaningless and without consistency.

For a clue to the inspiration of English work in the last quarter of the century, which embraces that of Charles' reign, that of James II and of William and Mary, it is advisable to turn a keen eye on the artistic and political actions of France.    The Great Louis was on the throne, and the great Le Brun was the leader in the decorative art of the day.

One of the political mistakes of Louis XIV was the Revocation of the Edict of Nantes, that edict which had protected from persecution so large a number of Protestant workers in the liberal arts. Among these people were tapestry weavers, silk weavers, glass workers, wood carvers, members of all the crafts that contribute to the beauty of the home.    Eventually they came to England for safe haven.

It is impossible to over-estimate the benefit to England in an æsthetic way of the advent of all these skilled workers, men whose equal were to be found in no other country.    Louis XIV had made a royal hobby of exquisite furnishings.    He had placed their manufacture among the royal pleasures and also among the state duties.    He had glorified the art of furnishing as it had never before been done, by the magnificent institution of the Gobelins factory. Here men learned their craft—an infinite variety of crafts—and achieved perfection.    All at once many of these workers were forced to flee or meet death under the new dictum of the King. And thus England received the outcasts to her own enrichment.

One of the industries in which England was behind the Continent was the manufacture of silk. The French refugees were soon established in London at Spitalfields, reproducing the magic weaves they had formerly made for the imperious pleasure of the royal favourites in France. Satins, brocades, taffetas of wondrous dye and lustre, flowed from the looms of the able weavers who thus drowned their nostalgia in excess of a loved and familiar occupation.

One result of this mass of beautiful material being thrown to a delighted public, was the change made in the fashion of interior wall-treatment. The beautiful oak panelling of other days oppressed with its seriousness the light mood of Charles II and his light companions. The gay sheen of silk was more sympathetic and enlivening. On the walls, then, went the silk. In Anne's time the panels grew larger, then became a wainscot and sank to the height of a man's bewigged and capricious head; then lowered to a chair's height for the Georgian era. And above flowed the gracious lines of silken fabrics concealing all the walls, made in Spitalfields by the French refugees and their followers.

The pretty Duchess of Portsmouth had her rooms hung with silk and with wondrous tapestries from

France, though England made both silks and tapestries. Beds of the day retained the high posts and tester or canopy, heavily draped, and the bed was similarly covered. The bed was carved, even to the tester, in French inspiration, and was elegant indeed. In such a bed came the King at last to lie in mortal illness in the palace at Whitehall, where the lovely Louise had first place by the royal invalid, while the Queen was treated as a negligible quantity. The Duchess of Cleveland, that other favourite, was not far in the background, and the King in his last hours remembered still another when he implored: "Don't let poor Nell starve."

# CHAPTER V

## THE END OF THE SEVENTEENTH CENTURY

### WILLIAM AND MARY. 1689–1702

THE style named for William and Mary embraces all the changes that occurred from late Carolean days until the time of Anne, and even includes some of the models and details that are given the name of that queen. Dutch influence comes largely into both, but was stronger in the style known as Queen Anne's. Mixed up with other influences were those not only of Holland but of the countries with which her political life was concerned. Spain contributed certain details, and as for the Dutch connections with the Near and the Far East, they supplied an infinity of inspiration.

Nothing more piquant to the decorative spirit could be imagined than the fantastic motifs of Indian and Chinese importation. To us, surfeited as we are from babyhood with Chinese toys and Indian stuffs, it is hard to look upon these things as startling novelties. But in those days of less travel they were delicious exotics. Among persons of fashion, there was a rage for the living evidences of the strange East, and more than popular as pets in the drawing-

Plate XXIV—INTERESTING CHAIR TRANSITIONAL BETWEEN STUART
STYLES AND WILLIAM AND MARY

CHAIRS IN VARIANTS OF WILLIAM AND MARY
Covered with petit point of the time

WILLIAM AND MARY CANED CHAIRS, ONE WITH FLUTED SPANISH
FOOT

Plate XXV

room became the exotic monkey and the vivid parrot. If these creatures, leashed to a standard, could be tended by a tiny black human, then fashion was pleased to an infantine joyousness.

Every ship that came in from far Eastern countries brought wise parrots and tiny frisking monkeys, and these were valued by decorative artists for models, as well as by my lady to pique gay conversation in her drawing-room.

William and Mary styles, like all of the seventeenth century, are at present in high vogue in America, and for this reason it interests us to study them. They come in after the use of oak has passed its vogue, and when walnut prevails, although woods of lighter colour, such as pearwood and sycamore, are employed. In chairs and sofas, carving prevails as decoration; but in cabinets and tables, the preference is for veneer and for inlay.

At this time occurs a change in the style of cabinets. Hitherto they had been closed cupboards; now, because of the fashion for collecting Delft china from Holland, a need came for cabinets that would display the collector's treasure. As furniture makers ever express the whims and needs of the day, so they at once invented the cabinet with shelf-top protected by glass. A feature of the design is the hooded top, so characteristic of William and Mary.

Two types of carving prevailed in chairs in the last twenty years of the seventeenth century, that of the broken C curve, originating under Charles II, and that of great elaboration which in some respects caught its details from the French. A study of the plates will show that the post-like upright which flanks the back is retained in both cases. Examples of fine carving under William and Mary show the free fancy of the designer and the skill of the worker who was possibly the designer as well. But the original chairs must be seen to gain any idea of the beauty of colour and finish. The whole bears the look of bronze that has been polished with caressing hands for centuries.

The shape of the leg in these finely carved chairs is to be noticed, as it is fathered by the chair-leg in vogue under Louis XIV in France, and in slight variations it prevails all through the William and Mary period. It is noticeable by a pear-shaped enlargement near the top. The Spanish foot is often seen on this style.

Petit point, gros point, or mere cross-stitch embroidery you may call it, was a fashionable occupation for dame and damsel. In Charles II's time the stuffed high-relief stump work pleased the court. Sorry stuff it looks now, much like the court ladies of that time, in that its colour and gilt are gone and its false art is pitifully exposed. But the good honest embroidery in wool and silk still stands, and is again tremendously in vogue.

It was Madame de Maintenon who gave such in-

Plate XXVI—CHEST OF DRAWERS IN BURR WALNUT VENEER
Mounted on legs, used in the last quarter of the XVII century

Plate XXVII—SMALL WALNUT TABLE

With spiral legs and inlay. Here is seen the beginning of the flat serpentine stretcher

spiration to the work in France that England copied. Her school at St. Cyr, which she conducted solely for the purpose of giving happiness and education to penniless daughters of fallen aristocrats, at that school the young girls executed work that ranks with objects of art. A well-known American collector has a large sofa executed thus under the hand of Madame de Maintenon which represents scenes from a play of Molière's, the piece having also been given by these same young girls, then the cartoons drawn by an artist of high talent.

So petit point was almost a high art in France in the time of William and Mary, and England did her best to follow the fine pattern set her. If, in judging whether this work be French or English, the mind hesitates, it is well to take the eye from the medallions and study how the designer filled the big field outside. In French drawing the whole is a harmonious composition; in the English, the hand is crude and uncertain, and the motifs meaningless, though bold, without coherence or co-ordination. Nowadays the lady who wishes to embroider a chair gets from Paris a medallion already complete and fills in the surrounding territory at her pleasure. It would seem that the ladies in England did the same in the seventeenth century, but with less taste.

Among minor points of interest, those little points used by the amateur in identifying, is the marked change in the stretcher. Away back in the beginning of the century, as seen on chairs and tables, it was heavy, made of square three- or four-inch oak, and placed almost on the ground. The first change was in using thinner wood; the next was in giving the stretcher a look of ornamental lightness by turning. When this happened the front stretcher of chairs was lifted from the ground to spare it the heavy wear apparent in older pieces. When carving attacked the stretcher, then it was placed well out of the way of harm, and it took on the ornamental effect of the chair's back. The Portuguese style of stretcher copied closely the carving on the top of the back in graceful curves.

It was when the larger pieces of furniture took on a certain lightness of effect that a change in their stretchers occurred, and this was in the period of William and Mary. The stretcher became wide, flat and serpentine. In chairs it wandered diagonally from the legs, meeting in the centre. In tables its shape was regulated by the size of the table top. In chests of drawers it wavered from leg to leg of the six which like short posts supported the weight. If the piece of furniture was inlaid these flat stretchers offered fine opportunity for continuing the work.

Strangely enough the stretcher, in chairs at least, disappeared at just the time it was most needed. That was at the introduction of the curved or cabriole leg, in the early days of Queen Anne. Those who know by experience how frail the curve makes

Plate XXVIII—CARVED CHAIRS.   PERIOD OF WILLIAM AND MARY
With all the fine characteristics of the carved designs of the time

Plate XXIX—WALNUT CHAIRS, WILLIAM AND MARY
With the exquisitely carved backs, stretches and legs characteristic of the time

this sort of construction, sigh with regret that the fine old Queen Anne pieces of their collection cannot be consistently stayed according to the older method.

It was in the interesting time of William and Mary that the kneehole desk made its appearance. A certain enchanting clumsiness marks these desks from later products on the same line, and a decided flavour of Chinese construction. Such a desk was recently rooted out of the dark in an obscure Connecticut town, it having been brought over in the early days, and, not being mahogany, has lain despised by local dealers until one more "knowledgeable" than his fellows discovered that it was Elizabethan!

A contribution made by China was the art of lacquering. Although it was not in the fulness of its vogue until the century had turned the corner in Queen Anne's reign, it had its beginnings in the earlier importations of lacquer and the desire of the cabinet-makers to imitate the imported art.

Varnish as we know it had never been in use, else had we missed the wonderful hand polish on old oak and walnut that cannot be imitated. And when it appeared it was only to use it in the Chinese manner, as a thick lacquer over painted or relief ornament. As the art of lacquering grew, cabinets of great elaboration became fashionable, and these were in many cases imported from China as the cunning handicraft of the Chinese exceeded that of the English in making tiny drawers and tea-box effects. Then these pieces were sent to England where they were painted and lacquered by ladies as a fashionable pastime, and were set on elaborate carved stands of gilt in a style savouring more of Grinling Gibbons than of China, —which is the true accounting of the puzzling combination of lacquer and gold carving.

The metal mounts or hardware of furniture throughout the seventeenth century was simple beyond necessity, yet this simplicity has its charm. In earliest days, iron locks and hinges of a Gothic prudence as to size and invulnerability, ushered in the century, but it was still the time of Shakespeare, and that time threw a glance back to the Gothic just left behind.

Knobs were needed as drawers appeared, and these were conveniently and logically made of wood, and were cut in facets like a diamond. But the prevailing metal mount for the rest of the century was the little drop handle that resembles nothing so much as a lady's long earring. It is found on old Jacobean cabinets, side-tables, and all pieces having drawers and cupboards. Its origin is old Spanish, and that smacks always of Moorish. With unusual fidelity this little drop handle clung until under Queen Anne (1703) the fashion changed to the wide ornamental plate with looplike handle, and *that* in turn served, with but slight variations, throughout the century.

In summing up the seventeenth century as a whole, it seems to show a British and insular attempt

**QUEEN ANNE SINGLE CHAIR**

Made of walnut with carved motives gilded. This type of chair shows the strong effect of Chinese motifs, especially on the legs

**QUEEN ANNE ARM CHAIR**

Upholstered in gros point with splat black, and Dutch shell on curved legs. *Metropolitan Museum of Art New York*

**WALNUT QUEEN ANNE CHAIRS**

With carbriole leg and claw and ball foot adapted from Chinese Spanish leather set on with innumerable nails elegantly covers the taller. These chairs foreshadow the Georgian styles

Plate XXX

Plate XXXI—QUEEN ANNE CHAIR
With marquetry back and carved cabriole leg with hoof and serpentine stretcher
*Courtesy of P. W. French*

to form its own styles, to dress its homes and palaces in a British way, regardless of what the world elsewhere was doing. Bits of outside product came drifting across the Channel, but these were not treated with too great seriousness. They were never adopted intact with all the feeling of foreign thought shining from their elegant surfaces, but rather were cut apart and certain bits were used to tack onto the more British work. And it is just here that is found the secret of the charm which lies in old English furniture. It is the endeavour of England to tell her own story, and her story is necessarily different from that of France, Portugal, Spain, Holland, the East. So, although she borrows motifs from foreign lands, it is only to indicate her historical connection with them and not to make a witless copy of their wares.

This holds true even at the time when two great artists dominated the decorative arts in Europe, Rubens and Le Brun, and that decorative monarch, Louis XIV, ruled art as well as politics. Yet the insularity of England kept her, happily, from realising the fine flowering of French art to imitate it, and, instead, she expressed her own sturdy characteristic development.

And so we love the evidences of sincerity and the pursuit of beauty that our English ancestors made for us, and in our homes of ease, with these things about us, we like to dream of the men and women who created and used these dignified time-kissed old pieces. And in dreaming we forget the frailty and cruelty of courts and rulers and think on the nobility and courage of the lesser yet greater folk who laid the foundation of our country.

THE END